———∽∾∿———

EVERYTHING I NEEDED TO KNOW TO SUCCEED
I LEARNED AS A KID ON THE FARM

EVERYTHING I NEEDED TO KNOW TO SUCCEED I LEARNED AS A KID ON THE FARM

John T. Osterman, MBA, CLU, ChFC

Printed in the United States of America

Designed by Megan Katsanevakis
Illustrations by Penny Weber

Library of Congress Control Number: 2023921626
ISBN: 978-1-951568-39-9

SMALL
BATCH
BOOKS

493 SOUTH PLEASANT STREET
AMHERST, MASSACHUSETTS 01002
413.230.3943
SMALLBATCHBOOKS.COM

To my clients, to whom I owe everything—
thank you for your business and your friendship
and for letting me be part of your life.

To my clients, to whom I owe everything—
thank you for your business and your friendship
and for letting me be part of your life.

CONTENTS

PROLOGUE

THE SECRET SAUCE

———⟨⟨⟨⟩⟩⟩———

In the past few years, several good friends who were familiar with my career accomplishments have suggested that I write down my "secret sauce." What were the specific strategies, business philosophies, and business practices that I used during my financial planning career?

As I reflected on this project, I began to realize that a lot of the strategies were actually lessons that I had learned as a kid growing up on a farm in downstate rural Illinois. With that, I began to put pen to paper.

First, a few thoughts. This is all from memory. It is my interpretation of events and experiences that happened seventy years ago, plus or minus, so please take that into account. These are my impressions, my recollections—the lessons that have stayed with me.

But before I get into that, it is important, I think, to understand some of what those lessons helped to create, so I am going to give you a brief summary of my career and accomplishments, to serve as context for what comes later in the story.

On April 1, 1979—April Fools' Day—I was hoping that giving up my career as a manager for Braden Machinery, the local Caterpillar Tractor and John Deere dealer, and signing a contract to represent New York Life would not turn out to be a big April Fools' joke on myself. I was thirty-five years old, held a high managerial position at Braden Machinery, and, relatively speaking, was making an excellent salary with numerous benefits. My then wife questioned whether I was making a colossal mistake by giving up a guaranteed salary and trading that in for a 100 percent commission-based arrangement. It was a reasonable concern.

But I had a big, burning desire to be in business for myself. I gave changing careers much thought before I pulled the trigger. My business life up until then had always been as an employee. Going forward, I wanted to be compensated based solely on my production. I no longer wanted my compensation to be determined by anyone except me.

During my first year representing New York Life as a career agent, I qualified for Chairman's Council, their highest council club, which represents the top 2 percent of their sales force. It was a remarkable achievement and a tremendous start to my new career. About one out of every thousand agents qualifies for Chairman's Council in their first year of business. I was that one. And I knew at that moment that I had the possibility of creating a spectacular career for myself.

In my second year, and in all the following years, I consistently qualified for Chairman's Council—twenty-nine years in all. Being part of this distinguished core group of agents who year after year consistently qualified for Chairman's Council meant that I was continuously in the top one half of 1 percent of the New York Life sales force, which has the reputation as one of the most accomplished and respected sales forces in our industry. As a quick aside, by my third year in my new career, I had more than quadrupled my previous salary with Braden Machinery.

I was based out of Yuma, Arizona, and Yuma was always under the Tucson General Office. For most of my career, I led the New York Life Tucson General Office as their number one producing agent. For more than fourteen years, as an agent based in Yuma, I also led the entire state of Arizona as the top producing New York Life agent. When I first accomplished that feat, a few of the longtime big producers in Phoenix told me, "Congratulations, but this has to be a fluke," and they warned that it obviously was never going to happen again. They pointed out that the Phoenix metropolitan area was more than twenty times larger than Yuma and that Phoenix had all the wealth. By the third year of continuously leading the state of Arizona as the number one producing New York Life agent, these same agents had changed their tune. Now they wanted to learn about my "secret sauce."

About a third of the way through my career, New York Life decided, as a new business venture, to enter into the securities business. As a registered representative, I consistently qualified for the Eagle Strategies Plus category, meaning that my assets under management placed me in the top twenty producers of the New York Life Eagle Strategies division.

Most New York Life agents at some point in their career

have to make a decision whether to broker products outside of New York Life. I don't believe that there is an absolute right or wrong answer to this. Every agent has the right to choose his or her own business model. The career agents that do not broker typically follow a business model that affirms that New York Life is a very large, excellent, financially solvent company and offers a wide selection of products. In essence, they see no reason to broker. From the agent's administrative point of view, it is certainly much simpler not to broker. Other career agents take a different approach, and I was in that group. Our view is that, as good as New York Life is, no one company has all the best products, all the time, and in every market. And of course, there are some markets that New York Life does not serve.

I believed that there were certainly times when it was necessary and appropriate to broker business with a few other excellent companies. The overriding principle was that I worked for my clients. They were, in effect, my bosses. My clients were the ones who needed to understand, appreciate, and be satisfied with my recommendations. There are many factors that go into determining the very best product for each individual client, including age, gender, and health issues, to name a few. Only after the different insurance companies reach a decision regarding underwriting and pricing is it possible to determine the very best product for each client. I did not work exclusively for any particular insurance company. The point is, I represented different insurance companies so that I could select the very best products that fit the particular needs of my clients.

In addition to my New York Life business, my brokerage business also turned out to be very significant. One year I was the number one producing agent for Royal Maccabees Life Insurance Company. Not bad for a boy from Yuma. I continued to be a top agent for that company for about twenty-five years, as well as for Jackson National Life, where I was a top agent for about the same number of years.

Perhaps the most highly respected organization in the insurance and financial services arena is the Million Dollar Round Table. The top-tier level within that organization is referred to as Top of the Table. I qualified for the Million Dollar Round Table every year that I was in business, and I qualified for Top of the Table nine times. One out of every thousand agents worldwide representing all of the insurance companies has the necessary production to qualify for Top of the Table. I was thrilled to be in such rarified air!

Why am I recounting my accomplishments here? To impress you? Not at all. What I want to do is to impress upon you that the lessons I learned on the farm, and the strategies that I used as a consequence, formed the basis for my success. If you choose to adopt them, they can dramatically improve your production, your career, and your life. The opportunity is just waiting for you to act. If you want, you can be at the very top of your profession. The choice is yours. As you will soon learn, *you are either in or out.*

ONE

YOU ARE EITHER IN OR OUT

M y guess is that every farm kid in the Midwest and throughout our nation did some form of chores. At what age does the responsibility for chores begin? About as early as possible—probably as soon as a child is able to walk and talk and have an elementary understanding of instructions.

My first chore was feeding and watering the chickens and harvesting the eggs. Then I graduated to the big time! I would have been about six years old, and my new duties were feeding and watering the cattle and in general looking after them. Dad explained to me that this was a big deal—a big promotion. I would be responsible for the well-being of the cattle. This had to be done daily, every single day. The weather conditions did not matter. Whether it was snowing, raining, windy, or freezing outside was not important. What was important was that the cattle got fed and watered. In a nutshell, I couldn't control the weather, but I could control whether the chores got completed. Also, at least on the Osterman farm, chores needed to be accomplished the very first thing in the morning. Breakfast was served *only* after the chores were done.

Very early in the morning, Dad would wake me and tell me it was time to start chores. If it was winter, I would get dressed as warmly as possible, including overalls, a big jacket, a hat that covered my ears, gloves, and snow boots for my walk across the barnyard and into the barn. The cattle were on the lower level, and the haymow, where all the hay was stored, was on the second level. To get there, I would climb up a ladder that was permanently secured to the side of the interior wall of the barn and go through an open square hole in the haymow floor that was probably three feet by three feet. To dismount the ladder and land on the haymow floor took two separate maneuvers. First, I had to swing my legs and feet from the ladder. Then, simultaneously, I had to release my grip on the ladder and push out, forcing myself away from the ladder and toward the haymow floor. That had to be done right, or I would fall back onto the first floor. There were no second chances. OSHA had not even been conceived in the early 1950s. Had they been overseeing my chores, they would have been beyond horrified about the technique I just described to arrive on the haymow floor!

Once on the floor, the next step was to climb up a small mountain of hay toward the area above the hay manger, where the cattle were waiting below to be fed. Then, once I climbed down the mountain of hay, I secured the first bale of hay and dragged it toward the manger. I am kind of guessing a little on this, but when I was six, a normal bale of hay probably would have been as tall as and wider than me. I probably weighed about as much as the bale.

Once I manhandled—or more specifically, *childhandled*—the bale in place, I needed to cut the two cords of twine that held the hay bale together, so I would reach for my trusty pocket knife. It was a very important tool, but I could hurt myself with it, so Dad explained how to use it properly. By the way, it was a really big deal to be able to have a pocket knife at age six!

After I cut the two cords, the bale of hay came apart in slices, and that's what I would drop down into the hay manger. I would then manhandle another bale to the manger and repeat the process, probably using four or five bales in total for the feeding. The goal was to get the hay into the manger, completely filling it from side to side. Once that was done, I climbed back up the small mountain of hay toward the haymow exit—that is, the square hole in the floor. Descending the haymow required the same maneuvers, just in reverse. Again, there was no margin for error, as the consequences would be painful, and maybe even worse. Voilà—the first part of my chores, the feeding part, was successfully completed.

Next, I would walk to the cattle water tank in the barnyard. The first thing I had to do was break up the ice, and to do this, I would swing a crowbar over my head and crack it. Then I would use the crowbar like a cane to continue breaking up the ice into smaller pieces. I quickly learned to do this without splashing any cold water back on myself. So far, the chores involved a lot of physical effort—the manhandling of hay bales and breaking up of the ice. The next part was not physical. It was all about manual dexterity and persistency. It involved using matches to light the wick on the kerosene-fired heater of the water tank.

A quick word about the matches. Dad explained that matches were another very important tool and again gave me all of the safety instructions so I knew how to use them properly.

First, I needed to open the glass door on the heater and then strike the match to light the wick. That sounds pretty simple, and on mild, non-windy days, it could normally be done pretty quickly. However, on cold, windy mornings, this could prove to be a big challenge. I soon learned to cup my hands to protect the flame of the match and to get the flame on the wick as soon as possible. I had to take the glove off my right hand to properly handle the matches, and after some unsuccessful attempts to get the wick lit, it was imperative to get my glove back on because my fingers were turning into icicles. I put my gloved right hand into my coat pocket and did a little circular dance just to warm up a little bit. As soon as I could, I took my glove off to try again to get the wick lit. On the worst mornings, there could be multiple circular dances involved.

One of the instructions from Dad was to use the matches sparingly. However, the bigger lesson was that it didn't really matter how many matches were used on windy days. All that mattered was getting the wick lit. As soon as the wick was lit, I closed the glass door, turned the circular valve to get the kerosene flowing, and, bingo, the water tank heater was operational. It provided enough heat to keep the water tank above thirty-two degrees, which meant that the cattle could have access to and drink water from the tank all day long.

After my chores had been completed successfully, then and only then could I walk back to the house for some breakfast. Guess what Dad and I would talk about during breakfast? We

talked about how my chores went! Dad would want to know how many hay bales were used, was my pocket knife still sharp, did I have enough matches for tomorrow, and so on.

My key takeaways were that I was solely responsible for the well-being of the cattle (I really wasn't, of course, but I thought so at the time) and that meant daily, first thing in the morning, getting the cattle fed and watered. The weather was not an excuse, really nothing was an excuse. The only thing that mattered was getting the chores accomplished. I learned that on windy days, the number of matches I needed to light the wick did not matter. There was no upper limit. The only thing that mattered was that I got the water tank heater operational. I also understood the importance of being trusted with some new tools. The overall lesson in my mind was that I was solely responsible for taking care of the cattle. I was being trusted and depended on to get the job accomplished. And I was six years old.

STRATEGIES

The first strategies that I used to further my financial services career go back to those lessons that I learned when I was six years old doing chores. Let's begin with some background information: B-A-N-G!!! New York Life just fired its starting pistol. It's July 1, and the new race for the future council qualifiers is on. On June 30 of the following year, the race is over. The final production numbers on that date determine whether an agent has qualified for one of the councils and, if so, which one. Also, at the end of each council year, New York

Life announces the new production requirements to qualify for each council for the coming year. I would always look at the new requirements for Chairman's Council and think, *Wow! They really increased the number! Holy cow! That's a big number. How am I going to write that much business and produce those numbers next year?* In a few minutes, I would calm down and tell myself that I was going to produce those required numbers and qualify for Chairman's Council again, like I always had in past years. The solution was simple: I would just use the same strategies that I always used. If I did that, I would be fine.

To begin with, I would always take the required Chairman's Council qualification number, which is expressed in first-year commissions that the agent needs to produce in the twelve-month period, and divide that number by ten. Let's say the number to qualify for Chairman's Council is $200,000. (I know that number is significantly higher now—the point is, whatever the qualification number is, just divide by ten.) So $200,000 divided by ten equals $20,000. In my case, I knew that this was now the new minimum number I had to produce each month for the next twelve months. Why divide by ten and not twelve? Because I always wanted to over-qualify, or build a cushion for the actual number, in case of a last-minute production reversal. That way, I would still have more than enough to qualify for Chairman's Council. No one wants to work really hard all year and then have a last-minute production number reduced, knocking him or her out of Chairman's Council. This plan helps prevent that from happening.

Here are some critical points regarding the strategy for producing a minimum of $20,000 per month:

First, the $20,000 minimum was not a goal I *hoped* to achieve each month. It was a mandate! The $20,000 minimum per month was just like doing chores. It needed to be accomplished. Period. No excuses. The cattle had to be fed and watered. Period. No excuses. One could ask what did I actually do to produce the $20,000? The answer is that there are hundreds of books, reading materials, and online resources explaining in detail how to accomplish that. But in a nutshell, to produce business, in our industry, it all centers around three activities: 1. calling a qualified prospect and securing an appointment; 2. conducting an opening interview; and 3. conducting a closing interview. In essence, the answer is simple. To produce the minimum of $20,000 per month, just do enough of those three activities.

Second, track your progress daily. On any given day of any given month, I would know exactly, down to the last dollar, how much business production I had on the books for that month. I would know how much I had in underwriting and how many opening and closing interviews I had on the calendar. Look, if you don't know those numbers, then you don't really know where you stand. If that's the case, how can you possibly know if you're ahead or behind for the month?

Third, if in any month you are behind, instantly increase the three critical activities we just discussed. Start putting in more hours, work nights, work weekends, whatever is required. If I were behind, I would start to cancel planned business meetings and planned family outings. I would cancel any activity that wasn't one of the three critical activities. Incidentally, having to cancel a family outing is really tough duty. I would work very hard to avoid putting myself in that position. Question: How do you avoid having a bad year? The standard answer is to catch it and fix it in January. With this strategy, you can catch it and fix it every month all throughout the year, thus assuring that a bad month doesn't turn into a bad year.

Fourth, here is a heads-up on a situation that is bound to happen. There are periods when, as an agent, you are diligently doing all three activities, and the end result is that all you get are *nos*. No, not today; no, maybe later, and so on and so on. Remember the chores example, when attempting to light the wick on the water heater on a cold and windy day. I could use as many matches as needed. The key was to just keep persisting, and it would eventually happen. As an agent, just stick with doing the three critical activities, and only those three activities. It's exactly the same thing as attempting to light the wick. Remember! There is no upper limit on the number of matches you can use, and there is no upper limit on conducting these three activities. Simply stick with it. Just like I eventually got the wick lit, you will eventually write some business. It's all about the law of averages. On the other hand, there will also be times when you are diligently doing all three critical activities, and all you get are *yeses*. You get inundated with *yeses*! How fabulous. What a business!

Fifth, as a six-year-old kid, I took responsibility for watering and feeding the cattle and looking after them in general. At the time, I thought that I was solely responsible for their well-being. As a thirty-five-year-old, my responsibilities were immensely more important. I was responsible for the financial well-being of my family. I took that responsibility very seriously, and failure was not an option.

Sixth, to be clear, even while doing all of the above, there were occasionally months when I did not reach the required minimum of $20,000. That meant that the following month, I would start out on double time. All planned activities were canceled, and the only activities that I would conduct would be the three critical activities. It was an all-hands-on-deck situation.

Seventh, remember how the chores had to be accomplished first, and then and only then was it time for breakfast? That meant that, in the months I exceeded the $20,000 minimum, it was time for a little reward. It could be something as simple as taking the family out for a really nice dinner, or something more extravagant like an overnight getaway.

I started with the idea that the $20,000 minimum monthly production requirement was a goal and a commitment to myself, the key word being *commitment.* This quote from Pat Riley, the famous former coach of the L.A. Lakers and Miami Heat, always made great sense to me: "There are only two options regarding commitment. You're either in or out. There's no such thing as a life in between."

Get the cattle fed and watered. Get the wick lit. Get the $20,000 minimum on the books every month.

Basically, this is a pretty simple strategy, and it's fairly foolproof. If I could produce a minimum of $20,000 each month, I would qualify for Chairman's Council that year. That's the strategy I used, and it worked every year for twenty-nine consecutive years.

TWO

UNLOADING ON THE GO

———❦———

The next major learning experience for me as a kid growing up on the farm occurred just as I was turning fourteen. There is no question that this experience had an impact on my career as the owner of Osterman Financial Group. It started with the arrival of a huge new piece of very expensive farm equipment: an International Harvester model number 101 combine. By comparison, it dwarfed all the rest of our farm equipment. Dad was one of the very first in our county and surrounding counties to invest in this radical new technology.

In essence, this new combine, painted completely red, could harvest crops much more effectively than the then-current harvesting methodology. In the farming world, this proved to be a game changer. In just one pass through the cornfield, it could separate the ear of corn from the stalk, the husk from the ear, and then shell the corn kernels from the cob. In just one pass, starting with ears of corn on stalks in the field, we ended up with shelled corn in the combine bin. And this whole process for an ear of corn, from beginning to end, took maybe forty-five seconds. It was an amazing advancement in harvesting crops.

That fall, once the corn was ready for harvest, Dad tried out his new International Harvester 101 combine. After a few adjustments, the combine worked just as advertised. The operation manual stated that once the combine bin was close to being full, you signaled for a truck driver, the truck was then pulled alongside the combine, and both pieces of equipment were stopped. The combine operator began to auger out the shelled corn into the truck bed. This whole process took probably ten minutes. During this time, the operators had a chance to converse. They probably talked about how the local high school football teams were doing, how the Cubs were losing that season—"Oh well, maybe next year"—or how the Chicago Bears had an excellent defense, but the offense was underperforming. Some things never change!

About one week after harvest had begun, Dad and I were having breakfast and talking about how well the new combine was performing. Then Dad said we were going to try something different that day. He said we were going to "unload on the go" and not waste the ten minutes it took to transfer the corn from the combine to the truck bed with both vehicles stopped.

He said that when he, as the combine operator, saw that the corn bin was starting to fill up—maybe two-thirds full—he would signal me in the truck, and I was to pull up next to the moving combine. Dad explained that he would not stop the combine. He would just keep harvesting. My job, as truck driver, was to get close enough to the combine—maybe twelve to sixteen inches—and then stay even with the moving combine. In other words, I would be adjusting the speed of my truck to exactly match the speed of the combine. Then Dad, as the combine operator, would swing the auger out over the truck bed and turn the auger on, thus beginning to transfer the shelled corn from the combine into the moving truck bed.

I was pretty astounded. I asked a lot of questions and *what ifs*, like, "What if, while we are both moving, I get too close and hit the combine?" I had other *what ifs*, but Dad assured me that he had seen me operate the truck since I was eleven years old and thought that at fourteen, I had the skill for the job, that this could work, and it was certainly worth a try.

It's now after breakfast and we're in the cornfield, ready to try our "unloading on the go" experiment. I was plenty nervous. I was in the truck with my eyes constantly following the combine, waiting for Dad to stand up and waive his arm for me to pull up beside him. Soon he waved, and the race was on. I started the truck in low, which we used to call "granny," and then I shifted to second gear to get some speed up. Cornfields can be really rough, so I could only go so fast, but I quickly caught up to the combine. Next, I double-clutched and downshifted into granny, pulling really close to the moving combine, maybe twelve inches away. Then I positioned my truck's shotgun door across from the ladder that the combine operator climbs up. We had discussed that if I did that, the truck bed should be under the combine auger. Then all I had to do was just maintain my truck speed and hold that position.

After a few seconds, I could see Dad swing the combine auger out over my truck bed and begin to auger the corn into it. He only looked straight ahead, totally focused on harvesting while the combine auger was dumping the corn into the moving truck bed. The last thing you want to do is spill the corn on the ground. Now both vehicles were moving in unison through the field. Both vehicles' engines were bellowing, so there was no possible way we could talk with each other. Everything was done by hand signals. My total focus was just maintaining my position. It seemed like an hour had passed, but it had been only about six minutes or so. Finally, I saw Dad shut the auger off and swing it back to the combine.

At that exact moment, Dad looked at me for the first time and gave me a big smile and a big thumbs-up. Mission accomplished! I gave him back a big smile and a big thumbs up. Then I immediately pulled the truck away from the combine and breathed a huge sigh of relief.

We had just proven to ourselves that we could unload on the go. We never went back to the recommended conventional method of stopping vehicles and transferring the corn. Throughout the fall harvest and going forward, Dad and I would trade off jobs. At times, I would operate the combine and Dad would assume the trucking responsibilities. Each and every time after we unloaded on the go, there was always the exchange of big smiles and a big thumbs-up. Nothing was going to stop us now!

Later on, throughout the farming industry, combine operators and truck drivers started unloading on the go. The old way wasted way too much time.

At sunset, when it got too dark to harvest, we would take the equipment to our farm machine shop, which had lighting. Once there, we began the maintenance. We checked everything—air pressure in all the tires, water and oil levels, grease and oil when and where necessary. We walked around the equipment to check the belts and chains for wear and filled up the gas tanks. The key point was we wanted the equipment to be completely ready to go first thing in the morning. Once it was all accomplished, it was time to head to the house for some dinner.

In summary, the lessons I learned are as follows:

First, as any farmer knows, there are a finite number of days for harvest. If it gets too late in the season, the crop can begin to go to waste in the field—a real tragedy for any farmer. So it's essential to be as efficient as possible in order to get the job done before it's too late.

Second, the big red IH model 101 combine was designed for one and only one purpose, and that was to harvest, which it did very well. So the key lesson here was to keep the big red combine going through the field. Keep it harvesting. Daylight is a burnin'. The goal is to avoid stopping the combine from doing its job.

Third, it is essential to have the equipment in excellent operating condition. No farmer wants to be broken down in the field for need of repairs. Keep the combine harvesting.

Fourth, another obvious lesson is that it's possible that new technology can make significant improvements in the way something is done. The point is to be open to, investigate, and consider new technology that will assist you in your endeavors.

Fifth, when Dad and I each operated our equipment, we were totally focused, each with a specific task. Our combined action yielded the desired result, which was depositing shelled corn into the moving truck bed in an effective and efficient way. It was an excellent example of teamwork.

STRATEGIES

In applying these lessons to my career at Osterman Financial Group, I, the agent, am the big red combine. My one and only job is to produce—that is, to write the business. I need to be solely focused on the three critical activities that we have already discussed. A quick point of clarification on activities two and three, the opening and closing interviews: Large cases, from inception to closure, can take months and involve three, four, five, or more meetings with the clients, their families, CPAs, and attorneys. The key point is that your activities should always be focused on closing the case. To do this, the following strategies are important:

First, it is essential to delegate all other activities, as much as possible, to your staff. If you are doing some other activity, it's like being broken down in the field. You are not producing.

Second, look for ways to save time. For example, when I was talking with a qualified prospect, attempting to secure an appointment, I would always suggest that we meet in my office. I would explain that I had a large conference room, we would not be interrupted, and the potential client would have my full attention. Also, since my staff and computers were there, we could answer almost any question immediately. That way, we could have a very efficient and effective meeting. All of the above statements are accurate, but there is another major advantage for the agent. It is very time efficient. You avoid the travel time both to and from the offices. Also, it precludes other inevitable delays, such as waiting in the prospect's office before the meeting, being interrupted during the meeting, and so on.

Early on, I realized that meeting in my office for appointments was so important that if I kept getting pushback on it, it was reason enough not to make the appointment and to move on to the next qualified prospect. Incidentally, once the first opening interview was conducted in my office, there was never any question again about where we would meet. It was always just assumed that we would meet again in my office. After the qualified prospects became clients, I always made the effort to visit their offices and tour their facilities. As an example, I might do this while delivering a Christmas present. The overriding point is that all of our serious business discussions were held in my office.

Third, the following situation, if not handled properly, can be an enormous waste of time and can actually put you out of business. It will definitely happen to all agents at some point, and unfortunately, it happens more times than any agent wants or deserves. Say you have accomplished all three critical activities masterfully. The qualified prospect is in complete agreement with your recommendations. All systems are go, and there is every reason to believe that the case will be closed very quickly. And then, at the last minute, there is a huge deal-killing roadblock. It came out of nowhere. You, as the agent, have done everything extremely well, but now this case is just dead. Why did this happen? Well, there can actually be numerous reasons. As an example, the qualified prospect's brother just yesterday signed a contract to represent North-western Mutual Life Insurance Company, and the prospect cannot proceed with you because he believes it would devastate his brother. I know there are ways to handle this objection, but in my example, let's assume this case is lost. And in the real world, cases can—and do—get lost at the last minute. It's like getting kicked by a mule in the chest, followed by another kick to the head. It's really tough.

So going forward, agents can react differently to the situation. You could say, "This is so unfair." It's going to take some time to heal, to recover, and then, maybe later, you can start making some calls. An agent can take four months to recover, or four weeks, or four days, or four hours. Actually, the choice is yours. If you take four months, it could put you out of business. If you are serious about making Chairman's Council that year, you had better take four hours or less time. Any longer, and you are out of production. It's like the big red combine sitting idly in the field when it could, and should, be harvesting. The only solution is to realize that you did an excellent job on the case, but it just did not work out, and immediately continue with your focus on the three critical activities. Get right back up when that mule knocks you down.

Fourth, the big red combine was the newest and most improved technology of its day. With that in mind, I always purchased the newest, fastest, most efficient, and most reliable office equipment. If it's faster, more efficient, and more reliable, why are you not using it?

Fifth, don't forget that you are the big red combine, the most important piece of equipment in the operation—do what it takes to stay healthy so that you can perform at your best. It is like maintenance on your most irreplaceable piece of equipment.

Sixth, I would encourage and pay for my staff to attend all of the training that was available to them. Your staff is obviously such an important part of keeping an office running smoothly and efficiently, why wouldn't you offer them all the support you can?

Seventh, here is another idea we employed every one to three years. We would bring in outside consultants to review Osterman Financial Group from head to toe. New York Life, through the Nautilus Division, offers consultants from their model office program. Also, there are numerous excellent independent insurance consultants outside of New York Life. The end result is that the consultants make recommendations, pointing out which areas in your operation are running well and which areas could be improved. It is a great way to assist you as you find ways to continually improve your practice, making it more efficient and effective.

Eighth, in order to achieve the required minimum monthly production, there had to be real teamwork between me, the agent, and my staff. We all needed to be totally focused on our separate tasks. My total focus was to write the business. My staff's total focus was to complete all of the required administration—getting the cases through underwriting and ready for delivery. The end result of this teamwork was production at the Chairman's Council level.

Bottom line: I was always looking for new ways to improve efficiency, using my "unload on the go" mindset.

THREE

IN THE FIELD AND ON THE FIELD

———⟨∞⟩———

My third lesson happened during my junior year in high school, playing football, and also impacted my future career. First, let me explain that I went to a small high school in downstate rural Illinois. My senior graduating class consisted of about fifty of us, as I recall. I lettered in the major sports, but the two sports that I excelled in were track and football. If I had gone to a bigger high school, however, who knows if I even would have made the team! My point is that my learning experience came about through how I prepared for the sport, not because I was a particularly great athlete.

Also, I should explain that the preparation all happened without any planning on anyone's part. It's just how the events unfolded. My parents said I could go out for any sport I wanted, but Dad, in particular, said I still needed to help as much as possible with the farm work. Our high school football practice was three times a day for about two hours per session. The practices were from 6:00 to 8:00 in the morning, then from

1:00 to 3:00 in the afternoon, and an evening practice from 6:00 to 8:00. These were held six days a week, with Sundays off, and continued for five weeks, starting the last week in July. The football practices at our high school were probably pretty much the same as those at the other high schools around us.

Because July and August are prime months for harvesting hay in rural Illinois, I knew I would be doing double duty—both football practice and baling hay. Here is how my schedule worked out: Every morning before I would leave for my first football practice, Mom would have already prepared a "to go" egg sandwich and a small bottle of milk for me to have on the way there. After the morning practice, I would immediately head to the designated hayfield and jump on a hay wagon.

Specifically, my job at the age of seventeen involved loading the hay wagon, which was being pulled through the field behind the baler and the tractor. The wagon was always bouncy, and the goal was to drag the bale from the hay baler and then start stacking it on the hay wagon. This involved lifting bales of hay about fifty pounds each over my head to complete the stacking of the hay wagon. Baling hay is hard, physical work, to say the least, especially during the hot and humid summer heat. Around noon, the wives took turns delivering lunch, so when it was their turn, Mom and my two sisters would bring some lunch out to the field for the hay crew. I would grab a sandwich and then head back to football practice, which started at 1:00. These early afternoon practices could be particularly grueling because they were held in the midday August heat. Right after practice, I would head straight back to the hayfield, jump on the hay wagon, and bale hay for the rest of the day until it was time to return to the evening football practice. After that final practice of the day, I would head directly to the A&W Root Beer stand and immediately down a half gallon of cold root beer, then head home, one exhausted kid. I was putting in hard fourteen-hour days, back-to-back, and knew that there were plenty more fourteen-hour days ahead. That root beer was my one treat!

So for the next five weeks, my entire life from early morning to late evening all centered around football practice and stacking hay bales on the wagon. At the end of those five weeks, I was in pretty darn good physical shape—not much body fat, and strong muscles.

Our football games were played in the fall every Friday night, and in our small community, they were well attended. Along with a good portion of the town's population, my family and relatives and neighbors all attended the games. So, of course, it was really important to me that I played as well as I could. Here is what I recall. It was the first game of the season. I was nervous and pretty uptight, and the game was about to start. As I looked at the opposition, I thought, *I think I'm pretty fast. I think I'm pretty strong. But what about them? Are they faster or stronger?* I knew that this game would be influenced by the desire to win—our coaches constantly pounded that thought into our heads—and I also thought it would depend upon how well we had prepared both individually and as a team. Basically, how hard and how well we had trained.

I'm looking at the opposition. They are doing pregame warm-ups just like we are. I feel pretty good about my speed and strength and desire to win—we will just have to see how that turns out once the game starts. I continue reflecting on the training aspect. Fundamentally, it is about the physical shape you're in, your stamina, and how very important that's going to be in this game. At that moment, I had a great insight, a big *aha*. As I'm studying the competition, I'm thinking, *Some of you may have trained as hard as me (actually, I knew most of them had not), but you sure as hell did not train harder than me, because in my mind that would be impossible—I had five weeks of hard football practice AND had baled a whole lot of hay.*

My confidence was growing. I began to feel less nervous, less uptight, realizing there was *no one* on the field out there who had out-trained me. I had trained as hard as anyone could. I was completely prepared. *So blow the whistle—let's start. I'm pumped. I'm ready. Blow the damn whistle, and let's get this game going!*

The lessons, of course, are first, that in any endeavor that is deemed important, being very well prepared is one essential element. Second, a big side benefit of being well prepared is that it naturally builds self-confidence. How important is self-confidence? If you answered, *It means everything*, good for you.

STRATEGIES

This is how I incorporated those lessons into my career at Osterman Financial Group: We have already discussed the three critical activities that an agent needs to focus on. The first one was contacting a qualified prospect with the goal of convincing him or her to schedule an appointment with me. I went into this activity *totally* prepared. If it was at all possible,

I had an existing client send the qualified prospect an introductory letter. I would find out as much as possible about the prospect before making the call. For example, for all of my prospects, I knew if they were married, how many kids they had, what type of business they were in, how long they had been in business, and primarily, how successful they were.

The next activity was the opening interview. I was also totally prepared for this. I knew exactly which questions I would be asking and in what order. I knew that I needed to listen intently and take excellent notes. I knew the goal was to have an in-depth understanding of the potential client's perspectives and priorities and what he or she thought was needed to accomplish their financial security.

The final activity was the closing interview. Again, preparation was key. I had thoroughly considered all of my recommendations. I used colored charts and diagrams to help visually explain my recommendations. I had anticipated all of the possible objections and was ready to respond to them all if necessary.

As we have discussed numerous times, these three critical activities are the only activities that the agent should be conducting. It should go without saying, then, that these three activities needed to be completed *successfully*. And in order to be successful, it is absolutely essential that the agent go into these three activities totally prepared. One final thought on this: When you do go into these activities totally prepared, you naturally exude confidence, which, as we said before, means everything.

FOUR

GIVING BACK

⁃⃝⃝

There was another lesson I learned as a kid growing up on the farm that impacted my financial planning career. Three or four times a year, between the planting and harvesting seasons, a pickup truck would pull into our barnyard. It might be just one farmer or, more often, two or three farmers together. They would ask me if this was the Theodore Osterman farm, I would say yes, and they would ask me if I could find my dad. These visits would always play out in the same way. Once I found Dad and told him we had visitors, he would greet them warmly. They would tell him where they were farming—which could be in our county or in neighboring counties. Then they would explain that they had heard that he was one of the best farmers in our county. They wondered if they could please ask him some questions. And then the questions began. What kind of fertilizer did he use, how much did he apply, and how often? How deep did he plant the corn, and how many kernels per acre, and so on. It was a continuous stream of questions.

Dad always responded very thoughtfully and took his time answering each question. At the end of the visit, which could last up to an hour, the farmers were always most appreciative. They would shake his hand, not once, but two or three times. I witnessed these types of meetings for probably ten years, from age eight to eighteen years old.

Early on, as a curious kid, I would ask Dad why he spent so much time with these people whom he didn't know and would probably never see again. I don't think I said it out loud, but what I was thinking was, *Why are you wasting so much time?* This was Dad's response: He told me that when he first started out farming as a young man, he would go to the successful farmers in our area and ask similar questions to those he had just been asked. And those farmers were always courteous to him and would answer all of his questions. So to Dad, it seemed fair, the right thing to do. He also said that all the questions made him think deeply about his responses, and sometimes he thought of ways to possibly improve his approach. Lastly, he said that during the conversations, he always learned something from the visiting farmers. Sometimes maybe just a little, and sometimes quite a lot. So overall, he felt that the conversations were good and worthwhile to have.

The lesson for me was in Dad's response. Giving back was the right thing to do, and the conversations could be win-win and worthwhile for everyone.

STRATEGIES

At least four months prior to signing on to represent New York Life, I thoroughly studied the insurance industry and, specifically, the job description of a career life insurance agent. Once I did sign on, I hit the ground running. I immersed myself in learning the profession, attended all the required courses, read numerous books, and so forth. I had already obtained my MBA and had become a Chartered Life Underwriter (CLU) and a Chartered Financial Consultant (ChFC) in rapid succession. Here are some strategies that I used both to learn from the experts and to pass those lessons along to others.

First, remembering the valuable conversations between Dad and the visiting farmers, and with the support of my general manager, I was able to interview very successful big hitters in our industry. These interviews proved to be extremely worthwhile in gaining insight into how they ran their practices.

Second, if you are a new agent and experience a lot of initial success, New York Life does an excellent job of shining the spotlight on you. As a result, I spoke at numerous New York Life General Offices. In addition to those presentations, New York Life asked me to speak at different venues, such as council club meetings. I thought that the speaking engagements, particularly with all the sidebar conversations, proved to be very worthwhile. A lot of agents, even sometimes years later, would tell me how my presentation really inspired them, and that as a result, they had adapted many of my ideas into their practice.

Third, let me share a particular event when I was asked to present that paid enormous dividends. This is how it unfolded: Phil Hildebrand, CLU, then the managing partner of New York Life's San Diego General Office, called me and said he had a proposal for me and really wanted me to seriously consider it. He proposed that he bring the top five producers in his General Office to visit me in my office in Yuma for the entire day. He suggested that in the morning I would give them a tour of my office and then speak at length as to how I ran my financial planning operation, specifically my strategies and business practices. Phil wanted all of the details and specifics. He proposed that in the afternoon, his top five producers would each present their best ideas, new concepts, and what they were incorporating into their practices. That would be followed by a group discussion on how the insurance industry was evolving, the new products being introduced, and so on.

I knew Phil well from previous meetings, respected him, and considered him a friend. I told him immediately that of course that sounded like an excellent way to spend the day, and we agreed on the date for their trip to my office.

After that meeting had concluded, I was completely energized. What an incredible day of sharing and getting invaluable insights! Like Dad said, we all learned from it.

The events from that day segue perfectly into the next chapter regarding the incredible benefits of being part of what the industry calls "study groups."

FIVE

PITCHING HORSESHOES AND PITCHING IN

I grew up in a small, tight-knit farm community. Many of my aunts and uncles and cousins were either neighbors or lived close by. In our community, we shared a lot. Clothes and toys got handed down. There were numerous potlucks and cookouts. Fresh sweet corn and tomatoes picked right out of our garden and eaten minutes later. The kids always seemed to find time for hide-and-go-seek, wrestling matches (for the boys), and catching lightning bugs in mason jars. The adults pitched horseshoes and enjoyed some friendly low-stakes poker games. All of us gathered for the ice cream socials. It was worth cranking the ice cream maker for what seemed like hours—nothing quite like homemade ice cream.

When it was time to work, we worked hard, putting in the long hours required to plant, tend, and harvest. We trusted each other. We had each other's backs. When a neighbor's hayfield needed to be brought in, we all showed up. Everyone took it as their personal responsibility to contribute. There were no slackers. Everyone pitched in.

From my perspective, life was pretty simple then. Pretty straightforward. Life was good.

STRATEGIES

After I had qualified for Chairman's Council in my first year, my managing partner, Terry Roberts, CLU, said he wanted some time with me. He reiterated what a remarkable accomplishment it was that I had qualified for Chairman's Council in my first year of business. But he continued. What about my second year in business? Believe me, that was also on my mind. I had had a burning desire to be in business for myself. Now I had an equally burning desire to make Chairman's Council again my second year.

Terry continued by saying that he thought I should seriously consider joining or forming a study group with like-minded agents. He explained in some detail the benefits and advantages. As I was listening to him, I had an immediate flashback. Joining a study group was going to be just like my experience of being part of a small, tight-knit farm community. Terry's advice was invaluable.

Participating in a study group is the only strategy that I am recommending in this chapter. It is that important. My good buddy and dear friend Ron Paulseen, CLU, ChFC, and I were the first two members of our newly formed study group. We immediately added three more members. At this writing, Ron and I have been in the same study group for forty-one years. For the past twenty-six years, our study group has been comprised of eleven members. We are all spread out across the country; three of us are retired, some are at different phases of their exit strategies, and the rest are still cranking the numbers. My ten fellow study group members could all easily qualify to be top members of the *Who's Who* in our industry. Each of them, without exception, either has had or is having a remarkable career. We are:

Arizona: John T. Osterman, MBA, CLU, ChFC
California: Ray Triplett Jr., CFP, CLU, ChFC
Illinois: Curtis T. Schultz
Illinois: Jerome A. Timmermann, CLU, ChFC
Kansas: Ronald V. Paulseen, CLU, ChFC
Massachusetts: Bradford L. Meigs, CLU, ChFC, AEP, MSFS
New York: Donald E. Lippencott, MSPS
Oklahoma: Michael R. Noland, CLU, ChFC, AEP
South Dakota: John P. Schwan
Wisconsin: Kamal N. Daya, CLU, ChFC
Wisconsin: Brian Ruh, CLTC

Looking back over my Osterman Financial Group career, the single biggest positive influence has been our study group. It is the number one most important thing I did. Remember, I have been doing it since my first year in business.

We take turns hosting our annual meetings, which usually last two or three days. We each make presentations in which we share everything, ranging from our newest business practices and how we see our industry developing to how our personal lives are evolving. We talk about our families and our communities. We share from our hearts. There are no secrets. We trust each other.

One of our members, Ray Triplett Jr., recently summed up his thoughts regarding his membership in our study group. "I know I would not be here without you. Your friendship and the wisdom and creative ideas that I have learned from each of you over the years were, and continue to be, a true blessing for me, my family, and my former staff and clients." I believe that each study group member would agree with Ray.

This is my view of my fellow study group members: They are my brothers, my dear friends, my compadres. I observe every one of them as they go through their various stages—not only in business but, more importantly, in life. The key—the magic—is that I know who they are, who they *really* are, and what they have accomplished and are accomplishing. And they know me, they get me, they know who I am at the core. And I know who they are at the core. So we have this incredible history, and it's ongoing. What we have as a group is really rare and wonderful.

My closing statement at each study group presentation over the years is always the same: "I am immensely impressed with and inspired by each and every one of you. Each and every one of you amazes me. I am honored to know you all, and I am honored to be here."

WORK WORTH DOING

———⁂———

For more than a year before I signed my contract to represent New York Life, I knew I wanted to be in business for myself, but I had to find the right career. One of the best books on the subject is Richard Bolles's *What Color Is Your Parachute?* I extensively referred to this book in designing my ideal career.

After much thought, research, and study, I drew up a list of job specifications that described the perfect career for me. After I developed that list, it was just a matter of matching up which careers fit my personal career specifications. Here is a list of the more significant ones.

First, I wanted a career that would enable me to deal with professional people and business owners. One of the key benefits of our profession is that I, as the agent, get to choose who I want to work with. As it turned out, a good number of my major clients have become lifelong friends. What a fantastic benefit!

Second, I wanted my career to give me the potential to earn an excellent income. In our profession, the sky is the limit. My compensation was based solely on my production. I was the one who determined my compensation.

Third, I did not want a job that would require me to spend most of my time on the road and away from home. There were other careers that filled many of my criteria but could have involved some fairly significant travel, going from city to city with many overnight stays away from family. I had done some of that in my previous employment at Caterpillar Tractor, and with my new career, the travel was easily eliminated.

Fourth, I was looking for a challenge and an opportunity to grow. In order to provide our clients with the best products and services, we are required to engage in continuous study to stay abreast of the marketplace and the financial world. Over the years, I attended many workshops and read extensively. One superb book that I read multiple times was Dale Carnegie's *How to Win Friends and Influence People*, and I recommend it to you. In short, one of the things that I like best about this career is that it boils down to putting yourself through a daily self-improvement course. The more you improve, the more value you can bring to your clients. The more value you bring, the more your compensation increases. What a fabulous circle of events!

Fifth, I wanted a career that would let me decide when I wanted to work and when I might want to take time off to be with my family or to fulfill other personal goals. "All work and no play makes Jack a dull boy." But being able to choose when you can play is a luxury that few people enjoy. This job specification proved to be most valuable to me. After I was in business for a while and had fine-tuned my business strategies, it was not uncommon for me to have produced that year's Chairman's Council requirements in the first eight or nine months of the council year. Wow! My chores were done, and I still had three or four months before my council year ended. During that time, it was my choice to throttle back a little bit. The key words are *my choice*.

My wife, Pam, and I took full advantage of having this choice. As one example, we both love to cruise the oceans and took numerous and relatively long trips. One of our favorites was the transatlantic cruise on Cunard's *Queen Mary 2*. It's a fabulous ship. We could do all of this because the chores were done first.

Imagine me, as an employee working for some corporation, saying to my bosses, "I have all my required work done for the year, and now I'll be taking off for a few months, including going on a month-long cruise" . . . and saying that every year. Any idea how that might go over?

Last, I wanted to be in a profession that would give me a sense of pride and have a positive influence on society. I believed then and, years later, remain firmly convinced that there is great value in what we do. We advise our clients and provide products and services that help them protect themselves, their families, and their businesses. We advise and offer solutions that assist them with their financial security. We can, and do, help our clients solve complex and critical problems. The families of many of my clients have allowed me to serve multiple generations.

This excerpt from a letter is typical of the gratitude that is expressed by many clients and their families. The son of one of my elderly clients sent it to me:

By the way, Mom asked me to say "hi" to you. She fondly remembers the great help that you gave Dad and her when they lived in Yuma. When I reviewed the information you gave me yesterday with Mom, she got tears in her eyes. She said, "Never in my wildest dreams did I think I'd have this much money. Your Dad would be so proud." By frugality, yet living a fun and valued life, and through wonderful assistance from you, they were financially secure, and Mom remains so today. Again, John, thanks for all of your help.

I made the right choice for myself, and I think I did that because I took the time to develop my ideal job description. I encourage you to make the effort to develop a list of job specifications to define your ideal career. Most of us spend the bulk of our years in some profession. That being the case, why not design your own perfect career?

In my case, it worked better than I ever could have dreamed. I look back upon my career with great pride and much satisfaction. I've always believed, and believe even more now, that this is an honorable profession.

I will end by borrowing from Theodore Roosevelt: "Far and away the best prize that life offers is the chance to work hard at work worth doing." That pretty much sums up this book.

ACKNOWLEDGMENTS

—————⌘—————

To my Dad—my best friend and most influential mentor, whose long shadow figures prominently in every chapter of this book. Thank you, Dad, for the life lessons I learned at your side.

To my Mom—thank you for your love, affection, and support, and for helping me find my educational path.

To my children and grandchildren—with the hope that you will understand the lessons of the farm and will use them in your careers and lives, whatever you choose to do.

To my two former employers, all of my managers at Caterpillar Tractor Company, including the CAT dealers I called on as a CAT rep, and Frosty Braden, owner of Braden Machinery Company—thank you for teaching me the ropes and how to be successful in the business world and in life.

To my New York Life managing partners and their staff, home office personnel, and my dedicated office staff at Osterman Financial Group—thank you for all of your support, insight, and encouragement throughout my career.

To Danny Taylor, CLU, ChFC, my New York Life managing partner for many years—thank you for your continuing support and advice, and for the invaluable assistance in editing this manuscript.

To Joe Lau, CLU, ChFC, my successor in business and my partner in my five-year exit strategy plan—thank you for entering our partnership as a close associate and ending it as a very good friend.

To Ron Watson, my good buddy and dear friend of five decades—thank you for encouraging me to write about my "secret sauce."

To my wife, Pam—thank you for all the brainstorming, listening, and encouragement for this endeavor. You are the wind in my sails and the best part of all our adventures.

www.ingramcontent.com/pod-product-compliance
Lightning Source LLC
Chambersburg PA
CBHW031910200326
41597CB00012B/575